SYDNEY, AUSTRALIA

TRAVEL GUIDE

2023-2024

Unveiling the Perfect Itinerary, Budget Tips, Must-See Activities, and Where to Stay

Henry Shaw

Copyright © by Henry Shaw 2023-2024

All rights reserved.

Except for brief quotations used in critical reviews and other noncommercial uses permitted by copyright law, no part of this publication may be copied, distributed, or transmitted in any way without the publisher's prior written consent, including by photocopying, recording, or other electronic or mechanical methods.

The use of any trademarks or brands mentioned in this book is solely for the purpose of clarification and is not intended to imply any affiliation with the respective owners of those marks or brands.

TABLE OF CONTENTS

INTRODUCTION
CHAPTER 1
What To Expect
    Climate
    Culture
    Customs
CHAPTER 2
Practical Informations
    Visa
    Currency and Exchange Rates
    Transportation Option Across Sydney, Australia
    Additional Useful Informations
CHAPTER 3
Planning Your Trip
    Best Time to Visit: Seasonal Consideration and Festivals
        Summer (December to February)
        Autumn (March to May)
        Winter (June to August)
        Spring (September to November)
    Budgeting for Your Sydney Adventure
    Recommended Itineraries: Making the Most of Your Time in Sydney
        7-Day Schedule
        10-Day Schedule

    14-Day Itinerary
CHAPTER 4
Exploring Sydney Cities
    Royal Botanic Garden
    Sydney Harbour Bridge
    The Rocks
    Circular Quay
  Hidden Gems of Sydney
  Tours and Activities in Sydney
CHAPTER 5
Discovering Sydney's Natural Wonders
  Natural Wonders and Scenic Routes
    Royal National Park
    Bondi to Coogee Coastal Walk
    The Gap and Watsons Bay
    Sydney's Northern Beaches
  Coastal Adventure: Exploring Sydney's Stunning Coastline
CHAPTER 6
Experiencing Sydney's Culture
  Cuisine: Sydney Food Scene
    Fresh Seafood
    Chinatown
    Street Food
  Art and Design: Sydney's Creative and Innovative Spirit
  Festivals and Events: Celebrating Sydney Traditions and Culture
  Language: Tips for Communicating with Sydney

Health and Safety: Staying Safe and Healthy While Traveling in Sydney
CHAPTER 7
Nightlife And Entertainment in Sydney
- Bar and Nightclubs
  - Kings Cross
  - CBD and Darling Harbour
- Theater and Cultural Performances

CHAPTER 8
Shopping
- Best Shopping Places in Sydney
- Local Boutiques and Market in Sydney

CHAPTER 9
Sydney Family Adventure
- Family- Friendly Attractions
  - Sea Life Sydney Aquarium
  - Darling Harbour
  - Bondi Beach
- Child-Friendly Accommodation
- Tips for Traveling with Kids

CHAPTER 10
Outdoor Adventure In Sydney
- Beaches and Water Activities
- Hiking and Nature Reserves in Sydney
- Affordable Activities and Eateries
- Free or Low-Cost Attractions
- CONCLUSION

INTRODUCTION

Welcome to the dazzling shores of Sydney, Australia – a city that needs no introduction yet never ceases to amaze. In this travel guide, we embark on an extraordinary journey through the heart of the Emerald City, revealing its hidden treasures, iconic landmarks, and the vibrant tapestry of experiences that await you.

Sydney is a metropolis that effortlessly blends natural wonders with urban sophistication. From its world-renowned Sydney Opera House and Sydney Harbour Bridge to its golden sandy beaches and lush coastal landscapes, this city is a symphony of sights, sounds, and tastes that captivate the senses.

But Sydney is more than its postcard-perfect exterior; it's a living, breathing entity with a multicultural heartbeat. It's a place where the past seamlessly melds with the present, where art and culture flourish, and where gastronomic delights from around the world converge.

Whether you're an intrepid adventurer, a culture enthusiast, or a foodie with a discerning palate, Sydney offers a cornucopia of experiences.

In the pages of this travel guide, we invite you to explore Sydney in all its glory. We'll navigate you through the labyrinthine laneways of The Rocks, take you on a journey across the mesmerizing Blue Mountains, and introduce you to the vibrant neighborhoods that give Sydney its unique character. From sunrise at Bondi Beach to twilight at the Opera House, every moment in this city is a brushstroke on the canvas of your memories.

Whether you're a first-time visitor or a returning friend, this guide is your key to unlocking the very best of Sydney. Discover the must-see attractions, uncover hidden gems known only to locals, and embark on unforgettable adventures that will etch Sydney into your heart forever.

So, pack your bags, prepare your senses, and get ready to dive into the kaleidoscope of experiences that Sydney, Australia, has to offer.

This is your passport to the unforgettable – your Sydney adventure begins now.

CHAPTER 1

What To Expect

It's important to be aware about Sydney's climate, culture, and customs before traveling there. The detailed summary that follows will help you prepare for your trip.

Climate

Sydney, Australia, has a great climate, making it a popular vacation spot all year round. In our Sydney Australia Travel Guide, we'll give you a quick rundown of the weather patterns and the ideal travel seasons:

Summer (December to February)

- Sydney's summer season lasts from December to February.

- Warm to hot weather with sporadic heat waves characterizes this season.
- The beach, outdoor recreation, and water sports are all quite popular at this time.
- Be ready, nevertheless, for sporadic summer storms.

Autumn (March to May)

- Sydney's springtime, which lasts from March through May, is temperate and comfortable.
- As the weather progressively cools, it is a fantastic time to go exploring outside.
- In certain places, the fall leaves enhance the natural beauty.

Winter (June to August)

- Sydney's winters are generally moderate, with temperatures seldom falling below zero.
- Budget tourists should take advantage of this period because hotel rates are frequently lower.
- Even if swimming is not recommended, you may still engage in tourist attractions and cultural pursuits.

Spring (September to November)

- From September through November, Sydney experiences spring, which is marked by a steady rise in temperature.
- The city is extremely beautiful as it blooms with vibrant flowers.

- The weather is perfect for outdoor activities and taking in Sydney's parks and gardens.

The ideal time to travel is mostly a matter of personal choice. Beach enthusiasts should choose the summer, while those who enjoy touring should choose the fall or spring. Although you could lose out on certain outdoor activities, winter can be a cost-effective choice. Sydney may get busy during the busiest travel seasons, so make travel arrangements appropriately.

Additionally, to be ready for any unforeseen changes in the environment, always check the most recent weather forecasts before your travel.

Culture

Sydney, Australia, is a thriving and multifaceted metropolis with a diversified cultural landscape that reflects its history, inhabitants, and surrounding landscape. You may maximize your trip by learning more about Sydney's cultural characteristics according to our travel guide.

- **Aboriginal Heritage:** Sydney is located in the ancient grounds of the Gadigal people, a part of the Eora Nation. Explore the Indigenous legacy by going to locations like the Royal Botanic Gardens, Aboriginal legacy Tours, or the Indigenous displays at the Australian Museum to fully comprehend the city's culture.

- **Museums and Galleries:** Sydney is home to a number of top-notch museums and galleries. A variety of art, history, and science exhibitions are available at the Australian Museum, the Museum of Contemporary Art, and the Art Gallery of New South Wales.
- **Performing Arts:** Sydney has a thriving performing arts community. A center for opera, ballet, and classical music, the Sydney Opera House is a landmark building. Major musicals are presented in the Capitol Theatre, while cutting-edge plays are presented at smaller venues like the Belvoir St. Theatre.
- **Festivals and Events:** Sydney holds a number of festivals all year long that honor everything from food and wine to movies and music. Events like the Sydney Film Festival, Vivid Sydney, and the Sydney Festival are must-attend ones that include both domestic and foreign talent.
- **Cuisine:** The city's ethnic populace has a significant impact on Sydney's

tremendously diversified cuisine scene. Fresh fish at the Sydney Fish Market and cosmopolitan fare in Leichhardt communities like Chinatown and Little Italy are just a few of the delectable options.
- **Coffee Culture:** Australians take their coffee very seriously, and Sydney is no exception. Visit neighborhood coffee shops and taste an iconic Australian coffee drink, the flat white.
- **Beaches:** A distinctive characteristic of Sydney is its seaside culture. Popular locations for surfing, tanning, and beachfront restaurants include Bondi Beach, Manly Beach, and Coogee Beach.
- **Outdoor Activities:** The city's outdoor culture promotes exploration and fitness. Take advantage of hiking in the Royal National Park or seaside walks like the Bondi to Coogee Walk.
- **Harbor Life:** Sydney Harbour is an important part of the city's culture. Visit the Taronga Zoo and have a picnic at the

Royal Botanic Garden, then take a ferry trip to take in the splendor of the port.
- **Diverse Neighborhoods:** From the ancient rocks of The Rocks to the hip vibes of Surry Hills, each Sydney suburb has its own distinct personality. You may get a taste of the different cultures of the city by exploring these locations.
- **Local Sports:** Australians have a strong interest in sports on a local level. Visit the Sydney Cricket Ground or Sydney Football Stadium to see a rugby, cricket, or Australian Rules Football match.
- **Nightlife:** Sydney boasts a thriving nightlife with a wide variety of bars, clubs, and live music venues. The nightlife is well-known at Kings Cross, Darlinghurst, and Oxford Street.

Keep in mind that Sydney's culture is always changing, so be willing to try new things and mingle with the people to fully experience the city's vibrant and cosmopolitan way of life. Have fun traveling in this fascinating Australian city!

Customs

Certainly! Australia's Sydney is a dynamic, multifaceted metropolis with a deep cultural legacy. Travelers to Sydney should be aware of a few traditions and etiquette to make their trip pleasurable and respectful of the local way of life. Key customs for a Sydney travel guide include the following:

- **Greeting:** Australians are kind and laid-back in general. A suitable greeting is a simple "G'day" or "Hello". Hugs and cheek kisses are less frequent in formal settings than handshakes.
- **Tipping:** Compared to some other nations, Australia does not tip as frequently. It is encouraged but not required. Before leaving a larger tip, confirm that service fees are typically already included in restaurant invoices.

- **Respect for Indigenous Culture:** Sydney is located on the Eora Nation's ancestral territory, which is respected. Respecting Indigenous heritage and culture is crucial. Consider participating in Indigenous cultural events while learning about the history of the area Native Americans.
- **Punctuality:** Australians admire punctuality, so it's a good idea to be on time for meetings, tours, and other scheduled events.

- **Beach Etiquette:** If you want to visit one of Sydney's stunning beaches, such as Bondi or Manly, keep in mind to observe customary behavior. Swim between the flags, follow lifeguard directions, and take sun protection precautions.
- **Dress Code:** Sydney is a multicultural city with a variety of fashion tastes. Although smart-casual clothes are suitable in more formal situations, such as fancy restaurants or theaters, feel free to dress casually.

- **Public Conduct:** In general, Australians regard kindness and politeness. Respect privacy, keep noise levels down in public areas, and abide by local regulations.
- **Age Requirement:** Sydney's drinking age is 18. If you want to buy alcohol, always have an ID on hand in case you need to provide proof of age.
- **Public Transportation:** Buses, trains, and ferries are all part of Sydney's enormous public transit network. For seamless travel, be sure to have an Opal card or contactless payment option.
- **Wildlife Respect:** Maintain a safe distance and don't feed any animals you come across in Sydney, such as kangaroos or wallabies. It's important to respect the environment of the unique and frequently protected species found in Australia.

Keep in mind that Sydney is a varied and welcoming city, therefore it is appreciated when people are respectful of and open to other cultures. You may make the most of your trip to

Sydney, Australia, by observing these traditions and advice.

CHAPTER 2

Practical Informations

Visa

Many people have a dream of visiting Sydney, Australia because of its magnificent beaches, well-known monuments, and dynamic culture. To guarantee a simple and hassle-free trip, it's essential to comprehend the visa requirements and application procedure before packing your bags and flying to Australia. You may use the information in this travel guide to get the visa you need for your trip to Sydney.

Types of Visa

Sydney, like the rest of Australia, provides a variety of visas to satisfy different travel needs. The most typical tourist visas are as follows:

- **Visitor Visa (subclass 600):** For quick excursions, such as family outings, business trips, and vacations.
- **Electronic Travel Authority (ETA) or eVisitor (subclass 651):** Available to nationals of qualified nations for leisure and business travel.
- **Working Holiday Visa (Subclass 417 and 462):** Travelers between the ages of 18 and 30 who desire to work and travel in Australia are eligible for the Working Holiday Visa (subclass 417 and 462).
- **Student Visa (subclass 500):** For foreign students attending Sydney-based universities.

Eligibility

Your country, intended use for the trip, and other considerations will all affect whether you are eligible for a Sydney visa. Make careful to verify the precise prerequisites for the visa category that best matches your needs.

Visa Application Process

Most visas for Sydney may be applied for online through the Department of Home Affairs' official website, which belongs to the Australian government.

- **Required Paperwork:** Prepare the essential paperwork, including your passport, passport-sized pictures, trip schedule, evidence of adequate finances, and any additional documents specifically needed for the visa you want.
- **Health Checks and Biometrics:** Some visa types may require you to visit a designated center for health examinations and biometric data collecting.
- **Visa Fees:** Visa costs Pay the correct visa fee, which varies based on the kind of visa and length of stay.

Process Duration

Depending on the visa type and the number of applications being handled, the length of time it takes to process your visa application may change. To ensure enough processing time, it is advised to submit your application well in advance of the day you want to travel.

Visa Expiration
Pay close attention to how long your visa is valid. Verify that your visa is valid for the entire time you will be in Sydney, and make note of any limitations or restrictions attached to it.

Observing visa requirements
Once in Sydney, it's important to abide by the terms of your visa, which include staying within the allotted time frame and not engaging in any unpermitted employment.

Getting a New Visa
Investigate your possibilities for extending your visa if you want to remain longer in Sydney. You might need to satisfy certain requirements.

Choosing the appropriate visa is a crucial part of arranging your trip to Sydney.

Make sure you thoroughly understand the visa criteria before applying, and follow the application procedure to the letter. You may look forward to experiencing Sydney, Australia's beauty, culture, and experiences now that the visa requirements are taken care of.

Currency and Exchange Rates

Understanding the local currency and conversion rates is crucial when making travel plans to Sydney, Australia, in order to efficiently manage your finances while there. You may learn about Sydney's local currency and how to deal with exchange rates from this tutorial.

Currency

The Australian Dollar, represented as $ or shortened as AUD, is the country of Australia's legal tender. It is frequently called the "dollar."

Denominations

Australian currency is available in a range of denominations:

$5 (blue)
$10 (purple)
$20 (red)
$50 (yellow),and
$100 (green) are the prices.

Coins with values of $2 (gold and silver), $1 (gold), 50 cents (silver), 20 cents (silver), and 10 cents (silver) are also often used.

Rates of exchange

Daily fluctuations in exchange rates are caused by a number of variables, such as interest rates, geopolitical events, and the state of the economy. You may check with the following for the most precise and recent exchange rates:
 - Local banks and currency exchange offices
- Online currency converters and financial news websites
- Mobile applications that display currency rates in real time.

Where to Find Currency Exchange

Several places in Sydney provide currency exchange services, including:

- **Banks:** The majority of banks provide currency exchange services, however they might impose fees or provide less favorable exchange rates.

- **Currency Exchange Bureaus:** Airports, retail malls, and popular tourist destinations all have a ton of currency exchange bureaus.

- **ATMs:** You may use your debit or credit card to withdraw Australian dollars from ATMs. However, you should be mindful of potential bank costs for currency conversion and ATM usage.

Cards - Credit

Travelers may easily use credit and debit cards in Sydney because of the city's widespread acceptance of them. Most people use Visa and Mastercard, then American Express and Discover, however these may not be accepted everywhere.

Fees for Currency Conversion

Be mindful of potential currency translation and international transaction fees when using credit or debit cards. For details on these costs, contact your bank or credit card company.

Currency Exchange Advice

Shop around for the best prices at several currency exchange offices.

- Have modest amounts of cash on hand in case a location doesn't take credit cards.

- To prevent card restrictions, let your bank know about your vacation intentions.

To manage your finances when visiting Sydney, Australia, you must be aware of the local currency and conversion rates. Make the most of your time in Sydney by staying up to date on exchange rates,
selecting the most affordable means of money conversion, and being informed.

Transportation Option Across Sydney, Australia

In Sydney, Australia, there are several ways to move about the city and its surroundings. Here are some of the most popular options for transportation:

Public transportation: Transport for NSW manages Sydney's enormous public transit system. It contains:

- **Trains:** Sydney trains The city and its surrounding areas are served by a large rail network.
- **Buses:** Buses go on routes that serve suburban and regional communities that are not served by railroads.
- **Ferries:** Sydney Harbour and Parramatta River both provide ferry services, making them a beautiful option for city exploration.

- **Light Rail:** The inner-western suburbs and other portions of the city are connected by the light rail network.

Opal Card: Get an Opal card, a smart card that can be loaded with credit and used on all Sydney public transportation systems, to make using public transportation more convenient.

Taxis and Rideshares: Taxis and ridesharing services are widely available all across Sydney, including Uber. They could be a practical choice for one-way trips.

Cycling: Sydney is a bike-friendly city since it offers bike lanes and trails in many locations. Bike rentals and bike-sharing programs like Lime or Jump are both options.

Walking: Seeing Sydney's sights on foot is a terrific way to do so, especially in the CBD and places like Circular Quay and Darling Harbour.

Car rentals: Although they aren't usually essential in the city, they might be helpful if you want to travel outside of Sydney.

Airport Transportation: Sydney Airport has excellent train, taxi, and ridesharing service connections to the city core. In order to get to the CBD quickly and conveniently, take the Airport Link rail.

Tourist Passes: If you want to use public transportation regularly, think about buying a MyMulti or MyPass card. These cards provide limitless travel for a predetermined time, which can help you save money.

Sydney Metro: Connecting several areas of the city and suburbs, the Sydney Metro is a fast transport system. It's a practical method to move about, especially in places where conventional railroads don't have good coverage.

Ferry to Manly: A popular and picturesque way to get to Manly Beach is by riding a ferry from Circular Quay to Manly.

Services for airport shuttles: Along with the train, there are a number of shuttle services that can transport you to and from the airport while accommodating a range of budgets and party sizes.

Due to Sydney's multiple transit choices, getting around the city and taking in all of its sights is very simple. You can select the form of transportation that best meets your requirements and tastes.

Additional Useful Informations

Certainly! Additional advice and details for a travel guide to Sydney, Australia are provided below:

- **Weather:** Sydney has a temperate temperature, but it's always a good idea to check the weather forecast before your trip. Winters (June to August) are colder and occasionally wet, whereas summers (December to February) are warm and can get extremely hot.

- **Transportation:** Sydney has a robust public transit network that includes buses, trains, ferries, trams, and other vehicles. Consider obtaining an Opal card for practical and affordable travel.
- **Language:** English is the official language, however due to the cosmopolitan nature of the community, you may hear a variety of accents.
- **Currency:** The Australian Dollar (AUD) is the unit of exchange in Sydney.
- **Credit and Debit card:** Despite the widespread acceptance of credit and debit cards, it's a good idea to have some cash on hand for smaller transactions.
- **Safety:** Sydney is a fairly secure city, but like with any large city, it's important to be alert of your surroundings and follow the usual safety precautions.
- **Time Zone:** Sydney does not follow daylight saving time and runs on Australian Eastern Standard Time (AEST), UTC+10.

- **Attractions:** The Sydney Opera House, Sydney Harbour Bridge, Bondi Beach, Taronga Zoo, and the Royal Botanic Garden are just a few of the famous places you shouldn't miss. For breathtaking city views, think about going on a harbor cruise.

- **Food & Dining:** The culinary scene in Sydney is diverse. Try some regional specialties including Tim Tams (chocolate biscuits), meat pies, and fish and chips. In various neighborhoods, you may also sample numerous international cuisines.

- **Events and Festivals:** Check the local events calendar for festivals, exhibits, and athletic events taking place while you are there. World-renowned New Year's Eve fireworks are displayed in Sydney.

- **Beaches:** In addition to Bondi, Sydney is home to several more stunning beaches, such as Manly Beach, Coogee Beach, and

Palm Beach. Each provides a special experience.

- **Shopping:** For the best selection, go to places like Paddington Markets, the Queen Victoria Building, and Pitt Street Mall.

- **Medical care:** Sydney boasts first-rate medical facilities, but it's a good idea to get travel insurance that includes emergency medical coverage.

- **Wi-Fi:** Free Wi-Fi is available in many Sydney cafés, shopping centers, and public areas.

- **Local Etiquette:** Australians are kind and laid-back people in general. Although not required, tipping is appreciated when receiving superior service.

- **National Parks:** For outdoor experiences and breathtaking scenery, visit adjacent national parks including the Blue Mountains and Royal National Park.

- **Local Wildlife:** Keep a watch out for the local fauna, which includes wallabies, kangaroos, and colorful birds.

- **Respect for Indigenous Culture:** Recognize and honor the indigenous heritage and culture of your area. To learn more about Aboriginal cultures, think about going on a cultural trip.

Always remember to tailor your itinerary to your personal interests and tastes, and have fun discovering Sydney's dynamic city!

CHAPTER 3

Planning Your Trip

Best Time to Visit: Seasonal Consideration and Festivals

Sydney, Australia provides a range of experiences all year round. Consider the following seasonal breakdown and important festivals while making travel plans:

Summer (December to February)

- The summer is the best time to visit because of the mild weather and the abundance of outdoor activities.
- Festivals include Australia Day celebrations on January 26 and the Sydney Festival, which takes place in January and features arts and music activities.

Autumn (March to May)

- Best Time to Visit: The weather is great for sightseeing due to the mild temperatures.
- Festivals include the Sydney Gay and Lesbian Mardi Gras (February–March) and the breathtaking light–and–music event Vivid Sydney (May–June).

Winter (June to August)

- Best Season to Visit: Winter is the best time to visit on a tight budget because it's off-peak. For individuals who like lower temperatures, it is also ideal.
- Festivals honoring French culture include the Sydney Film Festival in June and the Bastille Festival in July.

Spring (September to November)

- The best season to visit is spring, when flowers blossom and the weather is nice enough for outdoor activities.
- Festivals include Sydney Fringe Festival (September) and Sculpture by the Sea (October–November), which both include outdoor art works.

It's a good idea to check the forecast closer to your travel dates because Sydney's weather may be erratic. When deciding when to visit this dynamic city, keep in mind your own preferences for people and weather.

Budgeting for Your Sydney Adventure

It's crucial to set a budget for your trip to Sydney. Take into account costs for travel, lodging, meals, transportation, activities, and souvenirs. To help you budget effectively and control your spending while traveling, do some pricing research.

Recommended Itineraries: Making the Most of Your Time in Sydney

Certainly! Sydney, Australia, has a wide range of sights to see and things to do. To make the most of your stay in Sydney, consider the following two suggested itineraries:

Itinerary 1: Sydney Highlights (3 Days)

Day 1: Explore the City

- Start your morning tour to the Sydney Opera House at Circular Quay. You may either join a tour with a guide or just gaze at the magnificent building.
- Afternoon: After taking in the breathtaking views from the Sydney Harbour Bridge, visit the historic neighborhood of The Rocks.

- Dine at a Darling Harbour beachfront restaurant in the evening.

Day 2: Beaches and Coastal Beauty

- Head to Bondi Beach in the morning for a swim or a stroll down the coast to Coogee Beach.
- Visit the Bondi Icebergs Pool in the afternoon and have lunch at a seaside restaurant.
- Evening: Take in Bondi's exciting nightlife or return to the city for more eating alternatives.

Day 3: Sydney's Culture and Nature

- Visit the Royal Botanic Garden and the Art Gallery of New South Wales in the morning.
- Afternoon: Visit the historic Paddington district or travel by boat to Taronga Zoo.

- Evening: Have a picnic while watching the sun set over the Sydney Opera House in Mrs. Macquarie's Chair.

Itinerary 2: Extended Sydney Adventure (7 Days)

Day 1-3: According to the aforementioned "Sydney Highlights" plan.

Day 4: Blue Mountains Day Trip

- Visit the Blue Mountains for the day. Explore the beautiful woodlands and pay a visit to Scenic World and the Three Sisters.

Day 5: Hunter Valley Wine Region

- Take a tour of the Hunter Valley's wineries. Visit some of the best vineyards in the area and eat at a fine dining establishment.

Day 6: Coastal Adventure

- For hiking and environmental exploration, take a train or a car to the Royal National Park.
- Afternoon: Unwind at Cronulla Beach or tour Kiama or Wollongong, two coastal towns.

Day 7: Sydney's Hidden Gems

- Visit less congested destinations like Watsons Bay's beachfront walk or Cockatoo Island's World Heritage Site.
- Evening: Take a romantic dinner cruise on the harbor to roundferries off your journey.

Always verify the availability and opening times of attractions, and make reservations if necessary. You may travel conveniently with Sydney's public transit, which includes buses, trains, and . Have fun while you're in Sydney!

7-Day Itinerary

Day 1: Arrival and Sydney Harbor
- Touch down in Sydney.
- Take time to explore Sydney Opera House and Circular Quay.
- For famous vistas, cross the Sydney Harbour Bridge on foot.
- Dine al fresco at a restaurant on the harbor.

Day 2: Bondi Beach and the Bondi to Coogee Coastal Walk are among Sydney's beaches.
- Visit Bondi Beach to unwind or learn to surf.
- Discover the stores and eateries in Bondi.

Day 3: History and the Rocks
- Visit The Rocks, a historic location.
- Go to the Contemporary Art Museum.
- At the Hyde Park Barracks, learn about Sydney's history with convicts.
- Have supper at a bar by the water.

Day 4: Sydney's Cultural Life
- Go to the Art Gallery of New South Wales for the morning.

– Wander through the Royal Botanic Garden.
The Australian Museum should be visited.
- Check out a show at the Capitol Theatre.

Day 5: Visit the Blue Mountains for the day.
- Visit the Blue Mountains for the day.
- Visit the Three Sisters and Katoomba.
- Take in the sights of the Scenic World.
- Arrive back in Sydney that evening.

Day 6: Aquarium and wildlife
- Start the day off visiting Taronga Zoo.
- For spectacular vistas, take a boat from Circular Quay to the zoo.
- A visit to SEA LIFE Sydney Aquarium in the afternoon.
- Darling Harbour walk in the evening.

Day 7: Coastal Journey from Bondi to Manly
- Travel to Manly by ferry.
- Tour the Corso and Manly Beach.
- Walk the coastal path from Manly to Spit Bridge.
- Take a boat back to Circular Quay.

- On your final night in Sydney, eat at a restaurant with a view of the Opera House.

This tour provides a variety of Sydney's famous sites, as well as its natural beauty, history, and culture. Don't forget to verify the opening times and availability of attractions beforehand, and make sure to adapt it to your interests and speed. Enjoy your trip to Sydney!

10-Day Itinerary

Day 1: Entry into Sydney

- When you get to Sydney, check into your hotel.
- Discover the Sydney Harbour Bridge, the Sydney Opera House, and Circular Quay.
- Dine at a restaurant by the water.

Day 2: Sydney, Australia

- Visit Hyde Park and the Royal Botanic Garden.

- The Art Gallery of New South Wales is worth exploring.
- Take a stroll around the old town of The Rocks.
- Dine at a neighborhood restaurant to round off the day.

Day 3: Beach day

- The morning may be spent at Bondi Beach.
- Eat your lunch at a coastal café.
- Do the Bondi to Coogee Coastal Walk in the afternoon.
- Dine nearby and unwind on Coogee Beach

Day 4: Excursion to the Blue Mountains

- Visit the Blue Mountains for a day.
- Discover landmarks including Scenic World and the Three Sisters.
- Arrive back in Sydney that evening.

Day 5: Darling Harbour

- Check out the SEA LIFE Sydney Aquarium.
- The Australian National Maritime Museum is worth exploring.
- Dine while admiring the metropolitan skyline in Darling Harbour.

Day 6: Taronga Zoo

- Take a boat to Taronga Zoo and spend the day there.
- Experience animal interactions while exploring the zoo.
- For dinner, head back into the city.

Day 7: Manly day trip

- Travel to Manly Beach by ferry.

- Take a stroll to Shelly Beach and explore the beach.
- After lunch in Manly, come back to Sydney in the late afternoon.

Day 8: Historical sites

- Visit the Parramatta Historic District.
- Explore Parramatta Park and Old Government House.
- Eat supper at the dining district of Parramatta.

Day 9: Wine and Food

- Visit the Hunter Valley wine area for the day.
- Visit vineyards, delight in wine tasting, and have a meal there.
- After supper, head back to Sydney.

Day 10: Departure

- Explore any last-minute attractions or go shopping for souvenirs depending on when you are leaving.
- Go out of Sydney.

This program provides a variety of cultural events, natural splendor, and well-known Sydney monuments. Adapt it to your preferences and the time of year you're visiting. Have fun traveling to Sydney.

14-Day Itinerary

Day 1-2: Departure for Sydney
- Check in to your lodging.
- Views of the Sydney Opera House and Sydney Harbour Bridge may be had while exploring Circular Quay.
- Take a tour of the Sydney Opera House.
- Cross the Sydney Harbor Bridge on foot.
- Investigate The Rocks' historic district.

Day 3: Beach day
- Attend Bondi Beach for the day.

- Take a trip to Bondi Icebergs Pool.
- Enjoy eating on the sand.

Day 4: Taronga Zoo
- For a look at Australian animals, visit Taronga Zoo.
- From Circular Quay, take a shuttle to the zoo.

Day 5: Coastal stroll
- Participate in the Coogee to Bondi Coastal Walk.
- Take in the stunning seaside views.
- At Coogee Beach, unwind.

Day 6: Museums in Sydney
- Learn more about the Australian Museum.
- The Art Gallery of New South Wales is worth a visit.
- Darling Harbour in the evening.

Day 7: Blue Mountains

- Visit the Blue Mountains for the day.
- Discover breathtaking vistas and the Three Sisters.
- Arrive back in Sydney that evening.

Day 8: Manly Beach
- Travel to Manly Beach by ferry.
- Investigate Manly Beach's Corso.
- Unwind beside the sea.

Day 9: Wine tasting
- Visit Hunter Valley to sample wines.
- Lunch is served while touring nearby vineyards.
- Arrive back in Sydney that evening.

Day 10: The Neighborhoods of Sydney
- Discover Surry Hills' stores and eateries.
- For Newton's alternative culture, travel there.
- Nighttime on Oxford Street.

Day 11: Canberra day trip

- Visit Canberra, the nation's capital, for the day.
- Visit galleries and exhibits at the Australian War Memorial.
- Arrive back in Sydney that evening.

Day 12: Wildlife and the Beach
- Check out the Manly SEA LIFE Sanctuary.
- Visit Shelly Beach in the afternoon.
- Taronga Zoo's optional nighttime animal tour.

Day 13: Walk from Bondi to Bronte
- Bondi to Bronte Coastal Walk is a beautiful hike.
- Take advantage of the beaches you pass.
- Shopping and eating in the evening at Paddington.

Day 14: Goodbye, Sydney.
- shopping or touring that is urgent.
- Dinner is served at a beachfront restaurant as a goodbye.

- Go out of Sydney.

This itinerary includes a variety of Sydney's famous monuments, beaches, natural attractions, and cultural sites. Feel free to change it to suit your preferences and the time of year you're visiting. Enjoy the journey.

CHAPTER 4

Exploring Sydney Cities

Sydney exploration is a great adventure! You may tour areas including The Rocks, Darling Harbour, and Circular Quay, as well as famous sites like the Royal Botanic Garden, Sydney Harbour Bridge, and Bondi Beach. Don't forget to sample some delectable seafood and take in the lively culture of the city.

Royal Botanics Garden

Australia's Sydney Royal Botanic Garden is a magnificent and storied botanical paradise situated in the center of the city. It was founded in 1816, making it one of Australia's first scientific institutions as well as one of the nation's most recognizable parks.

The Royal Botanic Garden, which spans 74 acres, is home to an astonishing array of international plant species. Themed gardens with distinctive plant species on display in carefully maintained settings include the Herb Garden, Rose Garden, and Australian Rainforest Garden, which visitors may explore. The Calyx, a modern glasshouse that often holds exhibitions and activities about plants, science, and art, is one of the garden's highlights.

The Garden is a well-liked destination for both locals and tourists because it offers stunning views of Sydney Harbor, the Sydney Opera House, and the Sydney Harbour Bridge. The lovely grounds are the ideal location for outdoor activities like picnics and relaxation.

The Royal Botanic Garden is actively engaged in conservation initiatives, research, and teaching in addition to its horticultural marvels. It is actively involved in plant conservation activities, such as the preservation of endangered species, and plays a significant part in maintaining native Australian flora.

Visitors may also take part in educational events, workshops, and guided tours to learn more about the garden's abundant biodiversity and the cultural value of its plants. The Calyx frequently presents enlightening exhibits and activities that explore the interesting fields of botany, ecology, and sustainability.

Overall, Sydney's Royal Botanic Garden is a beloved haven of unspoiled beauty, cutting-edge research, and cultural enrichment. It still plays a significant role in defining Sydney's identity and serves as a reminder of the value of protecting and honoring the world's varied plant life.

Sydney Harbour Bridge

Sydney, Australia's magnificent skyline is adorned with the renowned Sydney Harbour Bridge. Due to its distinctive arch-based form, this great engineering feat is sometimes referred to as the "Coathanger" and serves as both a crucial transit route and a representative image of Sydney.

This steel arch bridge, which beautifully spans the clear waters of Sydney Harbour, is a monument to human creativity and inventiveness. Its hard economic times of the Great Depression saw the start of its construction in 1924, and on March 19, 1932, it was formally opened. In addition to serving as a symbol of hope during those tough times, the bridge provided work for a large number of people.

The Sydney Harbour Bridge is more than simply a way to cross the bay; it is also a popular tourist destination.

The bridge's highway, which is surrounded by eight lanes of traffic and two railroad tracks, makes it easier for people to travel and move products through the city on a regular basis. A special vantage point to take in the splendor of the harbor is provided by the designated walkways that allow walkers and bicycles to go along its course.

The stunning vista that the Sydney Harbour Bridge provides is among its most alluring features. The view is nothing short of captivating whether it is seen during the day or at night, when standing atop the bridge or from a distance.

The Sydney Opera House is framed by the bridge, forming an iconic pair that has come to represent the city. The bridge's lit arch and the city skyline make for a picture-perfect scene as the sun sets.

The Sydney Harbour Bridge has witnessed a variety of occasions throughout its history, including royal visits and spectacular fireworks displays during New Year's Eve festivities. It now serves as the focal point for important events and celebrations, representing Sydney's grandeur and passion.

Beyond its usefulness, the Sydney Harbour Bridge serves as a symbol of the tenacity of Sydney and all of Australia.

It is a living example of perseverance, development, and the quest of perfection.

Locals and travelers alike go to this location to admire the engineering wonder, take amazing images, and be in awe of the iconic structure's breathtaking beauty.

The Sydney Harbour Bridge is more than simply a structure; it is a steadfast representation of Sydney's character and a window into Australia's will and aspirations. For anybody visiting Sydney's bustling metropolis, it is a must-visit location because of its beautiful arches and breathtaking vistas.

The Rocks

In the center of Sydney, Australia, there is a dynamic and historic district called The Rocks. The First Fleet from Britain came here in 1788, marking the beginning of Sydney's European settlement, and it has a particular position in the city's history. The Rocks is now a fascinating destination for both visitors and residents thanks to how it integrates its historic past with contemporary attractions.

The Rocks' main attractions include:

Historic Charm: Cobblestone alleys, old structures, and winding lanes at The Rocks help to preserve the area's historic appeal and transport tourists back in time. You may visit places like Cadman's Cottage, Sydney's oldest surviving domestic structure.

Shopping and Dining: With a wide variety of boutique stores, art galleries, and eateries, the district is a hive of activity. At the various eateries, cafés, and pubs, visitors may browse for one-of-a-kind gifts, purchase original works of art, and sample a wide range of food.

The Rocks Markets: Rocks Markets are a must-go to if you're seeking handcrafted items, artisanal delicacies, and one-of-a-kind gifts. They take place every weekend. It's a great location to experience the local culture.

Museums and other Cultural Institutions: The region is home to a number of museums, such as The Rocks Discovery Museum, which chronicles the historical development of the neighborhood.

Harbour Views: Views of Sydney Harbour, the Sydney Opera House, and the Sydney Harbour Bridge may be enjoyed from The Rocks. Photographers and visitors looking for gorgeous panoramas frequently visit this location.

Festivals & Events: The Rocks holds several festivals and events throughout the year, honoring art, culture, gastronomy, and music.

Historical Tours: Guided tours are offered to dive into the area's history, including ghost tours that reveal fascinating tales from The Rocks' past. Particularly Vivid Sydney illuminates the neighborhood with breathtaking light works and performances.

Convict History: Through displays and guided tours, discover the challenges of the first convict pioneers.

Structures and artifacts constructed by convict labor shed light on this difficult era in Australian history.

The Rocks is a bustling, modern area with a distinct personality in addition to being a glimpse into Sydney's past. It is a must-visit location for anybody traveling to Sydney since it skillfully integrates history, culture, and entertainment.

Central Quay

At the northernmost point of Sydney's central business district (CBD), Circular Quay is one of the city's most famous and active waterfront areas. This thriving precinct serves as a transit hub as well as a center for aesthetic, recreational, and cultural activities. The following are some of Circular Quay's main attributes and draws:

Transport Hub: In Sydney, Circular Quay is a significant transportation hub. It serves as the main ferry port from which travelers may board vessels bound for a number of locations surrounding Sydney Harbour, including as Manly, Taronga Zoo, and Watsons Bay. Additionally close is the Circular Quay railway station, which offers quick access to the city's rail system.

Sydney Opera House: The Sydney Opera House is arguably the most well-known landmark that can be seen from Circular Quay. Its unusual sail-like construction makes it a global symbol in addition to being a Sydney landmark. From opera and ballet to concerts and theatrical shows, the Opera House accommodates a variety of activities.

Sydney Harbour Bridge: The Sydney Harbour Bridge is another well-known building that can be seen from Circular Quay. It's a breathtaking sight, especially at night when it's lit up. Atop the bridge, visitors may get stunning views of the city and port.

Cafés & Dining: A wide range of cafés, restaurants, and bars line Circular Quay. It's a great spot for dining with a view of the port and people-watching while sipping coffee.

Street Performers and Artists: Street performers and artists may frequently be seen in the neighborhood presenting their work. The quay is given a vibrant atmosphere by it, and artists of all kinds, from musicians to painters, may be seen showing their work.

Museum of Contemporary Art: Australia's top museum for contemporary art is the Museum of Contemporary Art (MCA), which is situated at Circular Quay. It provides visitors the chance to discover modern art in a lovely environment and showcases a diverse selection of shows that are always changing.

Overseas Passenger Terminal: Cruise ships land at the Overseas Passenger Terminal when they visit Sydney. Getting a close-up view of these enormous ships is astounding.

Ferry Rides: Beyond serving as a means of transit, Circular Quay ferry rides are a well-liked pastime in and of itself. From the sea, you can see the port, the city skyline, and famous sites.

New Year's Eve: Circular Quay serves as the focal point of Sydney's renowned New Year's Eve celebrations. Millions of people come to see the harbor fireworks show, which is a famous international event.

In addition to being a transit center, Circular Quay is a lively and scenic location where tourists can fully experience Sydney's culture, history, and natural beauty. Circular Quay has something for everyone, whether you're soaking in the stunning vistas, dining, or discovering the arts.

Hidden Gems of Sydney

Sydney is a city chock-full of well-known sights, but it also holds a few undiscovered jewels that provide uncommon and off-the-beaten-path experiences. Here are some undiscovered Sydney attractions to check out:

The Secret Garden of Wendy: This beautiful and peaceful garden was built by Wendy Whiteley, the widow of well-known Australian artist Brett Whiteley, and is conveniently located close to Lavender Bay and Luna Park. It's a serene haven with meandering walkways, artwork, and breathtaking harbor views.

Cockatoo Island: This UNESCO World Heritage-listed landmark is located in Sydney Harbor and provides an intriguing look into Australia's convict and nautical past. Campers may enjoy a variety of activities, including historical building exploration, entertainment, and art displays.

Barangaroo Reserve: Located on the western border of the CBD, Barangaroo Reserve is a recently constructed park with attractively planted green areas, walking paths, and picturesque harbor vistas. It's the perfect location for a tranquil picnic or leisurely walk.

Brett Whiteley Studio: The well-known Australian artist Brett Whiteley once resided and worked in this little museum nestled away in the Surry Hills district. It displays his artwork and offers details about his creative process.

Milk Beach: Milk Beach is a peaceful, gorgeous beach with excellent seas that is hidden away in the wealthy Vaucluse area. Swimming, picnicking, and admiring breathtaking views of the Sydney Harbour Bridge and city skyline are all highly recommended here.

The Royal National Park and Bundeena: The entrance to the Royal National Park is Bundeena, which is only a short boat trip from Cronulla. Discover the area's unspoiled beaches, coastal hikes, and the renowned Figure Eight Pools that are tucked away amid the rocks.

Cadmans Cottage: The oldest surviving residence in Sydney is called Cadmans Cottage, and it is located close to Circular Quay. Free guided tours are available, providing insight into early colonial life.

Chinese Garden of Friendship: Chinese Garden of Friendship is a peaceful haven with traditional Chinese buildings, koi-filled ponds, and beautiful gardens. It is situated in Darling Harbour. It offers a tranquil retreat from the busy city.

Glebe Markets: Every Saturday, the unique Glebe district hosts the Glebe Markets, which provide a wide selection of artisanal items, vintage apparel, handcrafted crafts, and delectable foreign street cuisine.

Lane Cove National Park: Just a short drive from the city, the national park of Lane Cove provides options for picnics, river kayaking, and bushwalking. It's the ideal getaway from the bustle of the city because of the tranquil surroundings.

These little-known facets of Sydney's culture, history, and natural beauty may be discovered through these hidden jewels. They provide a special viewpoint on what makes Sydney such a varied and interesting city.

Tours and Activities in Sydney

To accommodate a variety of interests and tastes, Sydney provides a wide selection of excursions and activities. You may enjoy the following excursions and activities in Sydney:

- **Sydney Harbour Cruises:** Take a picturesque tour on Sydney Harbour to view recognizable structures like the Sydney Opera House and Sydney Harbour Bridge. Lunch, supper, or sightseeing cruises are all options.
- **Sydney Opera House Tour:** Take a guided tour to learn more about the Sydney Opera House's stunning architecture. Learn about its development, history, and inner workings.
- **Taronga Zoo:** View a vast range of local and exotic species at Taronga Zoo, which is situated on the shores of Sydney Harbour. Additionally, you may take part in guided excursions and animal interactions.
- **Bondi to Coogee Coastal stroll:** Set out on a breathtaking coastal stroll that connects Bondi and Coogee beaches. Along the journey, take in the stunning beaches, rock pools, and ocean vistas.
- **Sydney BridgeClimb:** For sweeping views of the city and water, ascent to the

pinnacle of the Sydney Harbour Bridge. This tour provides a unique viewpoint of Sydney.

- **Blue Mountains Day Trip:** A day excursion to the Blue Mountains will allow you to see the Three Sisters rock formation, as well as lush woods and breathtaking waterfalls.
- **Hunter Valley Wine Tours:** Discover the Hunter Valley wine area on a tour with Hunter Valley Wine Tours, which is only a few hours from Sydney. Enjoy excellent culinary combinations while sipping wine at renowned wineries.
- **Manly Beach and the Northern Beaches:** Take a guided trip to discover Sydney's stunning northern beaches, which include Manly Beach. From Circular Quay, you may also board a ferry to Manly.
- **Sydney Fish Market:** Attend a cooking lesson or cuisine tour there to learn how to prepare fish. Learn about Australia's

varied marine life while sampling fresh seafood.
- **Surfing Lesson:** Lessons in surfing are available at Bondi Beach and other surf-friendly spots across Sydney.
- **Australian Museum:** Visit the Australian Museum to learn more about the country's natural and cultural heritage. It offers a variety of interactive exhibits and exhibitions.
- **The Rocks Walking Tours:** On a narrated walking tour, learn about the history of The Rocks. Discover its fascinating history, historic structures, and convict legacy.
- **Art Galleries:** To appreciate both Australian and foreign art, visit renowned institutions like the Art Gallery of New South Wales and the Museum of Contemporary Art.
- **Sydney Tower Eye:** From the viewing deck of the Sydney Tower Eye, take in 360-degree vistas of Sydney. It is

especially beautiful around dusk or at night.
- **Aquarium and Wildlife Experiences:** Visit the SEA LIFE Sydney Aquarium to discover the underwater worlds, and visit sites like Featherdale species Park to get up close to local Australian species.

You may fully immerse yourself in Sydney's culture, natural beauty, and distinctive attractions thanks to these excursions and activities, which provide a wide variety of experiences. Whatever your interests, Sydney has something to offer every tourist, whether they be in adventure, history, wildlife, or leisure.

CHAPTER 5

Discovering Sydney's Natural Wonders

Natural Wonders and Scenic Routes

Numerous natural wonders and scenic routes can be found in Sydney, Australia, including the Royal National Park, Bondi to Coogee Coastal Walk, Blue Mountain, Ku-ring-gai Chase National Park, The Gap and Watsons Bay, Hunter Valley, Manly Scenic Walkway, Sydney Harbour, The Royal Garden, and Sydney's Northern Beaches.

Royal National Park

The Royal National Park, an Australian natural treasure near Sydney, is renowned for its breathtaking coastline vistas, varied ecosystems, and deep Aboriginal heritage. It is the second-oldest national park in the world, having been founded in 1879.

This beautiful wilderness region is home to lush rainforests, precipitous cliffs, immaculate beaches, and an abundance of wildlife, making it a well-liked spot for hiking, picnics, swimming, and birding. The Coastal Track in the park provides beautiful views of the Pacific Ocean and chances to see local wildlife and flowers.

The local Aboriginal Dharawal people, who have a strong connection to the land and its history, view the Royal National Park as having considerable cultural importance in addition to its natural beauty.

This park is a must-see location for history historians and nature lovers alike since it offers visitors a wonderful combination of outdoor activities and cultural discovery.

Bondi to Coogee Coastal Walk

Sydney, Australia's outstanding 6-kilometer Bondi to Coogee Coastal Walk is known for its breathtaking ocean vistas, immaculate beaches, and dramatic clifftop scenery. This walk offers a stunning trek through some of Sydney's most beautiful coastal vistas, starting with the famous Bondi Beach and making its way to Coogee Beach.

Along the route, you'll pass through well-known locations with distinct charms and personalities, such as Tamarama Beach, Bronte Beach, and Gordon's Bay. The road winds through lush parklands where you can take in the natural splendor and find lots of places to rest and have picnics.

With cafés, sculptures, and historical sites strewn along the path, the Bondi to Coogee Coastal Walk is not only a great opportunity to admire

Sydney's natural beauty but also a chance to learn about the local way of life.

This coastal walk is a must-do activity when visiting Sydney, regardless of whether you enjoy the outdoors, the beach, or are simply looking for a relaxing stroll with stunning views.

The Gap and Watsons Bay

The Gap and Watsons Bay are two different but nearby Sydney, Australia landmarks:

The Gap:
- The Gap is a breathtaking coastal cliff that can be seen in Sydney's eastern suburbs, close to Watsons Bay.
- It is a well-liked tourist site because it looks out over the Tasman Sea and provides stunning panoramic views of the water.
- The steep plunge, which can be somewhat intimidating and at times rather awe-inspiring, and the cliff's rough beauty are its most well-known features.
- The Gap is renowned for its historical significance as well, and it includes a

memorial honoring those who perished there.

Watsons Bay:
- Watsons Bay is a quaint harborside neighborhood close to The Gap that is renowned for its natural beauty and laid-back vibe.
- It has beautiful beaches including Lady Bay Beach and Camp Cove that are great for swimming, picnicking, and sunbathing.
- The famous Watsons Bay Hotel, a historic inn with breathtaking views of the water, is also located in this neighborhood and is a well-liked place to eat and have a drink.
- Another notable feature of Watsons Bay is the adjacent Hornby Lighthouse, which provides breathtaking vistas and photo possibilities.

The Gap and Watsons Bay together provide a variety of scenic coastline vistas, outdoor activities, and natural beauty, making them well-liked travel destinations for Sydney residents and visitors alike.

Sydney's Northern Beaches

North of Sydney's central business district lies the magnificent and well-known coastline area known as Sydney's Northern Beaches. It is renowned for its unspoiled beaches, serene surroundings, and easygoing way of life. These are some of the main points:

- **Beaches:** Manly Beach, Palm Beach, Dee Why Beach, and many other gorgeous beaches can be found at the Northern Beaches, which are well known for them. Excellent surfing, swimming, and sunbathing possibilities may be found at these beaches.
- Manly: Manly is a bustling neighborhood and the entrance to the Northern Beaches. It is renowned for its vibrant surf scene, beautiful coastal hikes, and a lively waterfront district with lots of cafés, restaurants, and stores.

- **Palm Beach:** Known for its exclusivity and pristine surroundings, Palm Beach is the northernmost point of the Northern Beaches. Celebrities frequently visit this location, which offers breathtaking views from Barrenjoey Headland.
- **Pittwater:** Enjoy sailing, boating, and picnicking at this lovely inlet. It provides a distinctive fusion of outdoor leisure activities and natural beauty, offering a peaceful alternative to coastal beaches.
- **Bushwalks:** The Northern Beaches include a range of beach and woodland paths. There are several popular choices that offer breath-taking vistas of the coastline, including the Manly to Spit Bridge Walk and the Barrenjoey Lighthouse Walk.
- **Surfing:** The Northern Beaches are a popular destination for surfers of all skill levels because of their reliable waves. Those hoping to catch a wave may choose from a wide selection of surf schools and rental facilities.

- **Dining and shopping:** There are several restaurants and cafés in the neighborhood that serve fresh seafood and other types of cuisine. Additionally, you may tour marketplaces and boutique stores.
- **Relaxation:** The Northern Beaches provide a laid-back ambiance that enables you to unwind and enjoy the coastal lifestyle, whether you're searching for a quiet day in a beachfront park or a relaxed day at the beach.

The Northern Beaches of Sydney are a refuge for beach lovers, outdoor enthusiasts, and anyone looking for a peaceful respite from the bustle of the city.

Coastal Adventure: Exploring Sydney's Stunning Coastline

A fantastic trip that combines the beauty of the outdoors, outdoor activities, and a rich cultural experience may be had by exploring Sydney's breathtaking coastline. A more thorough explanation of this seaside trip follows:

- **Beach in Bondi:** One of Sydney's most well-known and energetic coastline locations, Bondi Beach, is a great place to start your tour. This beach's crescent shape makes it ideal for sunbathing, swimming, and people-watching. With the assistance of local teachers, you may also learn to surf here.
- **Bondi to Coogee Coastal Walk:** Set out on the magnificent 6-kilometer route that winds along the coastline known as the Bondi to Coogee Coastal Walk. You'll pass by spectacular landscapes, rock pools, and a number of gorgeous beaches, including Tamarama and Bronte. Hikers and those who enjoy the outdoors will welcome this chance.
- **Gordon's Bay:** Gordon's Bay is a remote snorkeling paradise and a hidden treasure along the Bondi to Coogee route. It is a distinctive location to discover marine life because of its underwater nature walk.
- **Bondi Icebergs Pool:** The Bondi Icebergs Pool is a famous oceanfront pool that is

close to Bondi Beach. Enjoy a lunch at the club's restaurant while taking a plunge while staring out at the Pacific Ocean.

- **Manly Beach:** Manly Beach is another must-see location farther to the north. Compared to Bondi, it has a more laid-back vibe and is ideal for beachcombing, picnics, and water sports.
- **Circular Quay to Manly Ferry:** Return to Circular Quay from Manly on a ferry to round up your journey. Stunning views of the Sydney Opera House, Sydney Harbour Bridge, and the city skyline are provided by this gorgeous boat trip.
- **Cultural Experiences:** While traveling along the coast, you'll also get the chance to learn about Sydney's rich culture. Explore neighborhood cafés, eateries, and art galleries to get a feel for the city's dynamic culture.
- **Safety and Conservation:** Keep in mind to use caution when exploring the shoreline. Pay attention to the waves, swim inside the flags at beaches that are

patrolled,and show respect for the surrounding animals and marine habitats.
- **Timing:** The Australian summer, which lasts from December to February, is the ideal period for this excursion because the temperature is mild and conducive to beach activities.
- **Transportation:** Access to these coastal locations is made simple by Sydney's effective public transit system, which includes buses and ferries. In addition, guided excursions and bike rentals are options.

Discovering Sydney's breathtaking coastline provides the ideal combination of outdoor leisure, natural beauty, and cultural immersion. Sydney's coastline has something to offer everyone, whether you enjoy the beach, hiking, or are just wanting to unwind by the water. This makes it a memorable coastal journey.

CHAPTER 6

Experiencing Sydney's Culture

Cuisine: Sydney Food Scene

Certainly! As a reflection of the city's multicultural mix and closeness to the water, Sydney's food scene is a culinary mashup. Fresh seafood, Chinatown, fine dining, café culture, beachside barbecue, multicultural fusion, street food, vegan and vegetarian options, indigenous Australian cuisine, wine, and craft beer are just a few of the options.

Fresh Seafood

As a result of its closeness to the Pacific Ocean and various coastal fishing settlements, Sydney, Australia, is known for its fresh seafood. Sydney's seafood scene has certain standout features, such as:

- **Sydney Fish Markets:** One of the largest seafood marketplaces in the world, Sydney Fish Market is famous for its wide

selection of fresh seafood, including fish, prawns, oysters, and more. Visitors have the option of eating at one of the on-site eateries or purchasing fish to take home.
- **Sydney Rock Oysters:** Sydney is well-known for its Sydney Rock Oysters, which are prized for their distinct flavor and superior quality. They are frequently served fresh or grilled with bacon and Worcestershire sauce (kilpatrick style).
- **Barramundi:** Barramundi is a well-liked fish in Sydney that is renowned for its delicate flavor and adaptability in the kitchen. It is frequently offered on restaurant menus and is a favorite among seafood lovers.
- **Prawns:** A classic in meals like prawn cocktails, grilled prawns, and seafood platters, Sydney's delicious prawns are available all year round.
- **Seafood Restaurants:** There are many different seafood restaurants in the city, ranging from fast food joints serving fish and chips to fine dining venues.

These restaurants frequently feature locally caught fish served in a variety of delicious ways.
- **Dining along the coast:** Outside of the city, coastal communities including Manly and Bondi Beach provide wonderful seafood dining experiences with seaside views, improving the whole gastronomic experience.
- **Sustainable Fishing Methods:** Sydney is dedicated to sustainable fishing methods in order to safeguard the fragile marine habitat for future generations. Responsible seafood procurement is prioritized by many markets and restaurants.

Sydney is a seafood lover's heaven with an abundance of fresh seafood selections for those who want to sample the best of the ocean.

Chinatown

Sydney's Chinatown is a thriving, culturally diverse district in the center of the city. It is one of the oldest and biggest Chinatowns in the

Southern Hemisphere and was established in the late 19th century. These are some of the main points:
- **Cultural Diversity:** The Chinatown in Sydney is a fusion of several Asian cultures, including Chinese, Vietnamese, Malaysian, and others. Its eateries, stores, and events all showcase this diversity.
- **Food Paradise:** It is known for its outstanding Asian food. Food Paradise. Chinatown provides a vast variety of gastronomic pleasures, including dumplings and noodles as well as exotic fruits and pastries.
- **Street Markets:** You may browse the crowded street markets to buy authentic souvenirs and traditional Chinese herbs and spices.
- **Architecture:** The area is a unique architectural attraction because it combines traditional Chinese building with contemporary Australian style.
- **Festivals:** Throughout the year, Chinatown is the site of a number of

cultural gatherings and events, including the Chinese New Year celebrations, which are marked by vibrant parades and performances.
- **Community Center:** In addition to drawing tourists, Chinatown is a flourishing neighborhood where locals and business owners uphold their traditions and heritage.

Sydney's Chinatown is not only a popular destination for food and culture, but it also exemplifies the multiculturalism and variety of the city.

Street Food

Sydney's street food is an enjoyable culinary experience that features a wide variety of flavors and ethnic influences. Here is a quick summary:
- **Multicultural Fusion:** Sydney's street food culture reflects the multicultural variety of the city. You may indulge in international cuisines including Thai,

Vietnamese, Lebanese, Mexican, and more.
- **Food Markets:** You may enjoy a variety of street delicacies from both domestic and foreign sellers at markets across the city such The Rocks Markets, Paddington Markets, and Carriageworks Farmers Market.
- **Iconic Snacks:** Meat pies, sausage rolls, and seafood dishes like fish and chips are among the must-try street foods from Australia.
- **Asian Delights:** Street food favorites including dumplings, noodles, satay, and buns are available in Sydney's Chinatown and Thai Town.
- **Fusion Food Trucks:** Food trucks are a rising trend, and many of them serve inventive fusion fare like Korean tacos, gourmet burgers, and handcrafted sweets.
- **Festivals of Culture:** Throughout the year, Sydney offers events and culinary festivals honoring various cuisines, giving

visitors the chance to sample delicacies from around the world in one location.

Sydney is a must-visit for food lovers eager to sample a variety of flavors directly on the city's streets because of its vibrant street food scene, which is a monument to the city's multiculturalism.

Art and Design: Sydney's Creative and Innovative Spirit

Sydney's culture and identity are strongly influenced by its creative and inventive spirit in art and design. Here are some important factors to think about:
- **Diverse Cultural Influences:** Sydney's multinational population has woven a complex tapestry of influences into the city's art and design. A distinctive and varied creative environment is produced by the fusion of Aboriginal art, Asian aesthetics, European styles, and other influences.

- **World-Class Galleries:** The Australian Museum, the Museum of Contemporary Art Australia, and the Art Gallery of New South Wales are just a few of the organizations that display an extraordinary collection of both domestic and foreign artworks. The limits of artistic expression are always being pushed by these places.
- **Emerging Artists:** Sydney's vibrant art community fosters new talent. Aspiring artists may hone their skills and try out new concepts at art colleges like the National Art School and the College of Fine Arts at the University of New South Wales.
- **Public art and street art:** Vibrant murals and installations covering walls and public places throughout Sydney's downtown streets, which serve as a canvas for urban art. This vibrant street art culture is a reflection of the city's modern and dynamic creative spirit.
- **Architectural Wonders:** Sydney is home to renowned structures like the Sydney

Opera House and the Sydney Harbour Bridge, two emblems of cutting-edge architecture. The city's skyline is evidence of its dedication to cutting-edge, environmentally friendly construction.
- **Fashion and Design:** Sydney's fashion sector is renowned for its creativity and sustainability. Local designers support environmentally friendly techniques, and fashion shows like Mercedes-Benz Fashion Week Australia present the most recent styles and trends.
- **Design festivals and events:** Sydney is home to a number of design festivals and events that highlight creativity via exhibits, installations, and hands-on activities.
- **Collaborative Spaces:** Co-working spaces and creative hubs like the Australian Design Centre provide designers and artists a supportive atmosphere to work together, discuss ideas, and push the limits of innovation.

- **Indigenous Art and Culture:** Through art and design, Sydney honors and celebrates its indigenous history. Indigenous art galleries and cultural institutions provide insights into the oldest continuously existing culture in the world, forging a stronger bond with the land and its legends.

Sydney's artistic and inventive attitude is a dynamic combination of traditions, cultures, and modern ideas. The city's dedication to developing talent, accepting diversity, and pushing the frontiers of artistic expression keeps it at the forefront of innovation on a worldwide scale.

Festivals and Events: Celebrating Sydney Traditions and Culture

Sydney is well recognized for its vivacious culture and varied customs, which are celebrated all year long with a range of festivals and events. Here are a few crucial ones:

- **Melbourne Festival:** The finest works of art, music, theater, and dance from across the world are presented at this yearly event, which is typically held in January. It's a wonderful way to begin the year with a cultural festival.
- **Vivid Sydney:** Vibrant Sydney Sydney's landmarks are lighted with breathtaking light shows in May and June, creating a spellbinding visual spectacle. It combines music, technology, and art.

- **Chinese New Year:** One of the largest Chinese New Year events outside of Asia is held in Sydney. In February, the city comes to life with lion and dragon dances, lantern parades, and great food.
- **Sydney Gay and Lesbian Mardi Gras:** One of the most well-known LGBTQ+ festivities in the world takes place during Sydney Gay and Lesbian Mardi Gras, which is held in February or March. There is a vibrant procession, as well as a number of events and performances.
- **Sculpture by the Sea:** Taking place in October along the picturesque Bondi to Tamarama coastal walk, this exhibition features sculptures by international artists against the backdrop of the breathtaking coastline.
- **NAIDOC Week:**NAIDOC Week is observed in July and features a variety of activities, such as art exhibits and

cultural presentations, to celebrate the history, culture, and accomplishments of Aboriginal and Torres Strait Islander peoples.
- **Greek celebration of Sydney:** In the middle of the city, the Greek community of Sydney holds a vibrant celebration in March that features Greek music, dancing, and delectable cuisine.
- **Sydney Film Festival:** In June, movie buffs get together for this occasion, which presents a wide selection of movies from all over the world, including Australian and Indigenous cinema.
- **Diwali celebration of Lights:** This event in October honors the Hindu celebration of Diwali and includes traditional Indian dancing, music, and an amazing light show at Parramatta.

- **Carols in the Domain:** A cherished Sydney Christmas custom, this free event in December comprises well-known musicians and choirs singing merry carols in a picturesque outdoor environment.

These are only a handful of the numerous festivals and events that honor Sydney's vibrant traditions and culture, which represent the multicultural richness of the whole city.

Language: Tips for Communicating with Sydney

Keep the following advice in mind when talking in Sydney to promote successful and courteous interactions:
- **Friendly Greetings:** Australians, notably Sydneysiders, are recognized for their friendliness. Initiate discussions with a grin and a formal salutation like "G'day" or "Hello."

- **Respect Personal Space:** Maintain a casual and laid-back tone in most settings since Sydney has a laid-back culture. Whenever you meet someone for the first time, use their first name.
- **Respect Personal Space:** Australians place a high importance on privacy, so keep your distance when speaking, especially to strangers.
- **Employ of Humor:** Australians frequently employ humor in conversation, so don't be hesitant to joke around or strike up a nice chat. But stay away from foul humor or delicate subjects.
- **Politeness Matters:** Saying "please" and "thank you" are common courtesies, and they are vital. Good manners and courtesy are valued in Australia.
- **Actively listen**: Australians value those who do this. Instead of dominating the discussion, pay attention to what others are saying and participate in it.
- **Beware of stereotypes:** Sydney is a multicultural city with residents from a

variety of origins. Respect various cultures and viewpoints and refrain from drawing conclusions based on stereotypes.
- **Time Sensitivity:** In Sydney, punctuality is typically anticipated. To respect people' time, be on time for appointments and meetings.
- **Use Clear Language:** Speak simply and refrain from using excessively formal or sophisticated vocabulary. Australians value openness in communication.
- **Local Slang:** Australians have their own distinct slang and idioms, despite the fact that English is the national language. To communicate more effectively with Australians, become familiar with some of their frequent terminology.

As Sydney is a cosmopolitan city, keep in mind that you may run into individuals from various origins. You will be able to communicate with Sydney residents more successfully if you are open-minded, courteous, and adaptive.

Health and Safety: Staying Safe and Healthy While Traveling in Sydney

Here are some health and safety recommendations to keep in mind when traveling, whether in Sydney or elsewhere:

- **Travel Insurance:** Make sure you have adequate travel insurance that covers unforeseen occurrences and medical crises.
- **Immunizations:** Before flying to Australia, find out whether you need to have any shots, and make sure your usual immunizations are up to date.
- **Sun Protection:** Australia has significant UV levels, therefore use sunscreen. For sun protection, put on sunscreen, sunglasses, and a hat with a broad brim.
- **Drink plenty of water:** Sydney may become hot. Stay hydrated by drinking lots of water, especially if you're spending time outside.

- **Traffic Safety:** When crossing the street, always look to your right since in Australia, traffic is on the left.
- **Emergency Number:** The local emergency numbers, including 000 for police, fire, and ambulance, should be memorized.
- **Water Safety:** When swimming in the ocean, use caution. Pay attention to strong currents and obey the lifeguard's directions.
- **Food and Drink:** Sydney's tap water is safe to drink, but if in doubt, stay with bottled water. Try the native cuisine as well, but be cautious while eating street food.
- **Protection from mosquitoes:** Mosquitoes might be bothersome depending on the season. In the nights, wear long sleeves, long trousers, and bug repellent.
- **COVID-19:** Keep up with the most recent COVID-19 requirements and limits. Observe the mask's rules and, if necessary, engage in social distance.

- **Travel Documents:** Store copies of your passport, visa, and other crucial documents apart from the originals in a secure location.
- **Local Laws:** To prevent any legal problems, familiarize yourself with the local laws and traditions.
- **Healthcare:** Although Sydney offers first-rate medical facilities, it is nevertheless important to carry travel insurance in case unanticipated medical costs arise.
- **Traveling Solo:** When traveling alone, give someone a copy of your itinerary and keep in regular contact with them.
- **Weather awareness:** Be ready for all kinds of weather. Particularly during Sydney's chilly winter months, plan your packing properly.

Always check for the most recent changes and regulations before and during your trip, keeping in mind that safety and health procedures might change. Have fun while you're in Sydney!

CHAPTER 7

Nightlife And Entertainment in Sydney

Bar and Nightclubs

Nightlife fans have a variety of alternatives in Sydney's bar and club scene. The bar and club scene in Sydney, including areas like Kings Cross, the CBD, and Darling Harbour, The Star Casino, Surry Hills, Darlinghurst, Circular Quay, and Newtown, is discussed in more length here.

Kings Cross

The ancient and well-known neighborhood of Kings Cross, sometimes known as "The Cross," is situated in the eastern region of Sydney, Australia. It has a long history of being a thriving entertainment area and the center of Sydney's nightlife. Here is some information on Kings Cross:

- **Historical Relevance:** Beginning in the early 20th century, Kings Cross had a thriving bohemian and creative culture. It became associated with counterculture movements in the 1960s and 1970s and served as a gathering place for artists, musicians, and authors.
- **Nightlife Hub:** Kings Cross has been known as Sydney's main nightlife zone thanks to the abundance of pubs, clubs, and entertainment establishments there. It was well renowned for having a nightly party atmosphere that drew both residents and visitors.
- **Iconic Landmark:** Several renowned monuments may be seen in the region, including the Coca-Cola sign that has come to represent Kings Cross. Another important feature nearby is the El Alamein Fountain.
- **Dining & cafés:** There are several restaurants, cafés, and eateries in Kings Cross that cater to a wide range of

preferences. It's a fantastic location for breakfast or a relaxed evening.
- **Transport Hub:** Sydney's Kings Cross train station is a significant transportation hub, making it simple to get to various areas of the city.
- **Currently:** Kings Cross still has a certain appeal, even though it may not be as associated with late-night fun as it once was. Some pubs and clubs are still open, providing a more laid-back and varied evening experience than they formerly did.

Kings Cross is still a vital component of Sydney's cultural landscape, and its evolution is a reflection of the city's changing goals and rules. Both tourists and residents may enjoy a night out at Kings Cross, whether they are interested in history, art, or a more somber occasion.

CBD and Darling Harbour

The core Business District (CBD) of Sydney and Darling Harbour are two core, busy parts of the city, each of which offers a distinctive experience and a variety of attractions. Here is a synopsis of each:

CBD, or central business district:
- **Financial Hub:** The business and financial center of Sydney is known as the CBD. It is one of Australia's most significant commercial areas and is home to large banks, global firms, and administrative offices.
- **Retail Paradise:** The CBD is home to a number of top-notch retail malls, such as Pitt Street Mall, which has the flagship stores of several worldwide and Australian companies. A gorgeous retail mall with boutique stores, the Queen Victoria Building (QVB) is noted for its architecture.
- **Cultural Attractions:** The Sydney Opera House and the Royal Botanic Garden are just two of the numerous cultural icons

that can be found in the CBD. In close proximity to each other are the New South Wales State Library and the Art Gallery.
- **Dining & entertainment:** There are a variety of restaurants in the region, from fine dining to laid-back cafés. There are various eateries with stunning harbor views on Circular Quay and The Rocks. Theaters like the Capitol Theatre also present a variety of performances and events.
- **Transport Hub:** Sydney's central business district is well connected to the rest of the city by a network of buses, trains, ferries, and light rail, making it simple to move around and go to other locations.

Darling Harbour:
- **Leisure & Entertainment:** Just west of the CBD lies the well-known leisure and entertainment district known as Darling Harbour. There are several family-friendly attractions available there, such as

Madame Tussauds, Wild Life Sydney Zoo, and SEA LIFE Sydney Aquarium.
- **Waterfront Views:** The port is a center for leisure activities and offers beautiful waterfront views. Visitors can enjoy boat rides and cruises or take leisurely strolls along the waterfront promenade.
- **Options for dining:** Darling Harbour is renowned for its diverse dining scene, which includes a wide variety of eateries, cafés, and pubs. You may savor international food while admiring the lovely surroundings.
- **Cultural Venue:** Australian National Maritime Museum, which covers Australia's maritime heritage, is one of the cultural venues in the region. Numerous occasions, conferences, and exhibits are held in the ICC Sydney (International Convention Centre).
- **Entertainment Complexes:** Harbourside Shopping Centre and Cockle Bay Wharf are two entertainment complexes in

Darling Harbour where you can shop, eat, and have a good time at night.
- **Fireworks Displays and Special Events:** Darling Harbour frequently hosts fireworks displays and other special events, especially during holidays and occasions like New Year's Eve.

Both the CBD and Darling Harbour provide a mix of commerce, culture, leisure, and entertainment, making them crucial stops for both visitors and locals in Sydney's dynamic metropolis.

Theater and Cultural Performances

Sydney has a thriving arts community with several theaters and cultural events. Several important locations and occasions include:
- **Sydney Opera House:** Opera, ballet, drama, and concerts are among the many acts held in the Sydney Opera House, which is renowned for its unique design.
- **Capitol Theatre:** The Capitol Theatre presents a range of live performances,

including concerts and Broadway-style musicals.
- **Belvoir St Theatre:** Australian theater shows that are cutting edge and modern are produced at the Belvoir St Theatre.
- **State Theatre:** Offers a variety of live acts, including as dance performances, concerts, and musicals.
- **Carriageworks:** Is a modern multi-arts venue that hosts exhibits, plays, and other cultural events.
- **Sydney Festival:** A yearly celebration of the arts that includes anything from theater and music to art installations.
- **Sydney Theatre Company:** Sydney Theatre Company is renowned for its top-notch theatrical productions, which include both traditional and modern pieces.
- **Art Gallery of New South Wales:** The Art Gallery of New South Wales occasionally presents cultural events and art-related exhibits.

- **Australian Museum:** Provides cultural programs and displays focused on the history and indigenous cultures of Australia.
- **Darling Harbour:** Throughout the year, it frequently holds outdoor cultural events, festivals, and performances.

CHAPTER 8

Shopping

Best Shopping Places in Sydney

Sydney has a vast selection of shopping opportunities, from busy markets to upscale luxury stores. Here are a few of Sydney's top shopping destinations.

- **Pitt Street Mall:** This pedestrian mall is home to the flagship stores of several worldwide and Australian businesses. It is situated in the center of the city.
- **Queen Victoria Building (QVB):** The stunningly preserved Queen Victoria Building (QVB) is home to upscale clothing boutiques, jewelry stores, and other businesses.
- **The Strand Arcade:** Another iconic retail district with a concentration on high-end and designer products is **The Strand Arcade.**

- **Westfield Sydney:** Is a sizable shopping center with a mix of high-end and high-street retailers as well as restaurants.
- **Paddington:** This hip neighbourhood is known for its boutique shopping, where you can discover distinctive clothing, housewares, and artwork.
- **The Rock:** A historic district with cobblestone streets and marketplaces where you may buy crafts, artwork, and mementos is The Rocks.
- **Sydney Fish Markets:** For fresh fish and gourmet goods, head to Sydney Fish Market if you're a culinary enthusiast.
- **Bondi Junction:** Is a retail center with a variety of fashion, beauty, and lifestyle businesses located close to the well-known Bondi Beach.
- **DFO Homebush:** This is a fantastic choice for outlet shopping and deals on well-known brands.
- **Glebe Markets:** These markets, which take place every Saturday, feature

homemade products, vintage apparel, and delectable street cuisine.

Before visiting these shopping areas, be sure to confirm the current operating hours. No matter if you're seeking high-end fashion or distinctive, locally manufactured goods, Sydney has something for every consumer.

Local Boutiques and Market in Sydney

There are many local markets and stores to discover in Sydney. Here are some well-known examples:

- **The Rocks Markets:** This market, which is situated in The Rocks' historic district, offers great food vendors as well as artisanal items and one-of-a-kind crafts.
- **Paddington Markets:** A must-visit for boutique shopping in Sydney,

Paddington Markets is known for its fashion, jewelry, and art.

- **Bondi Market:** Every Sunday at Bondi Beach are the Bondi Markets, where you can browse handcrafted goods, apparel, and jewelry.
- **Glebe Markets:** Glebe Markets are open on Saturdays and include vintage apparel, handcrafted crafts, and secondhand finds.
- **Newtown Market:** Visit the Newtown Market on Saturdays for retro and vintage goods as well as a lively atmosphere in the diverse area.
- **Manly Arts & Crafts Market:** This market along Manly Beach is open on the weekends and showcases goods made by regional craftsmen.
- **Kirribilli Markets**: The second Sunday of every month, the Kirribilli Markets near Sydney Harbour Bridge have upscale clothing, fine art, and gourmet food booths.

Keep in mind that market hours and days might change, so it's a good idea to look out their schedules online before making travel arrangements.Enjoy perusing Sydney's neighborhood stores!

CHAPTER 9

Sydney Family Adventure

Family- Friendly Attractions

Sea Life Sydney Aquarium, Darling Harbour, Wildlife Sydney Zoo, Sydney Tower Eye, Madame Tussauds Sydney, The Royal Botanic Garden, Taronga Zoo, Bondi Beach, and Featherdale Wildlife Park are just a few of the family-friendly attractions in Sydney.

Sea Life Sydney Aquarium

A terrific family-friendly destination near Sydney's Darling Harbour is the Sea Life Sydney Aquarium. What makes it a wonderful option is as follows:

- **Marine Adventure:** The aquarium provides a fascinating trip beneath the

surface. Families may discover a variety of aquatic life, including majestic sharks, vibrant coral reefs, and amusing penguins.
- **Interactive Exhibits:** Children may interact with interactive displays, such as touch pools where they can feel starfish and other aquatic life. Additionally, there are informative seminars and interactive displays.
- **Diverse creatures:** The Sea Life Sydney Aquarium exhibits a wide variety of marine creatures, giving kids the chance to learn about the seas and ecosystems of the world.
- **Underwater Tunnels:** The aquarium's amazing underwater tunnels are its main attraction. You will be surrounded by sharks, rays, and other aquatic animals as you move through these tunnels, making for a captivating and immersive experience.
- **Conversation Message:** The aquarium also emphasizes conservation initiatives, educating children about the value of

protecting marine ecosystems and the animals that call them home.
- **Accessibility:** Due to its handy location in Darling Harbour, it is simple to get to and combine with other nearby family-friendly activities.
- **Education Value:** Sea Life Sydney Aquarium is a great place to learn about marine biology and environmental protection since it provides educational programs and school field trips.
- **Family bundles:** To save entry expenses, look for family ticket alternatives and bundles.

It may become busy, especially on weekends and during school breaks, so plan to arrive early to avoid the crowds and have a more leisurely experience.

Darling Harbour

Offers playgrounds, museums, and restaurants.

Bondi Beach

Great for family beach outings and swimming.

Child-Friendly Accommodation

In order to make sure families have a good visit, Sydney offers a variety of family-friendly lodging options. Here are some alternatives to think about:

- **Family-Friendly Hotels:** Hotels that cater to families include several in Sydney and provide large rooms, cots, and kid-friendly features. Three well-liked options are the Novotel Sydney Darling Square, Shangri-La Hotel, and Four Seasons Hotel.
- **Serviced Apartments:** Apartments provide you more room and a kitchen, which makes it simpler to accommodate kids. Well-known choices include Meriton Suites and Adina Apartment Hotels.
- **Holiday Parks:** If your family prefers camping or cabin-style lodging, think

about staying at a holiday park like the NRMA Sydney Lakeside Holiday Park or Lane Cove River Tourist Park.
- **Kid-Focused Resorts:** The Fairmont Resort & Spa Blue Mountains and the Crowne Plaza Hunter Valley are two Sydney-area resorts that specialize in providing amenities and activities for kids.
- **Hostels with Family Rooms:** Budget-friendly hostels like YHA Sydney Harbour provide family rooms with private bathrooms, which are perfect for families traveling with young children.
- **Boutique B&Bs:** For a more personal experience, search for family-friendly B&Bs like Sydney's The Langham or Lurline House in the Blue Mountains.
- **Vacation rentals:** A large range of vacation rentals are available on websites like Airbnb and Stayz, which is a terrific alternative for families looking for a setting that feels like home.
- **Hotels with Pools:** Families with young children frequently stay at hotels with

> pools. Places like the PARKROYAL Darling Harbour, which boasts a rooftop pool with a view, should be taken into consideration.

Always look for features like family suites, play spaces, childproofing, and close access to family-friendly destinations when making a reservation. Read reviews left by other families to get a sense of how they found the chosen lodging.

Tips for Traveling with Kids

With little forward planning, traveling with children in Sydney can be a pleasant experience. Major pointers for making your family travel fun are as follows:
- **Create Children-Friendly Activities:** Zoos, aquariums, and parks are among the family-friendly activities you should research and prioritize. Sydney offers a variety of ways to amuse kids.

- **Childproofing the space:** If childproofing is offered, ask for it if you are staying in a hotel. Bring any essential kid safety supplies, such as outlet covers or corner protectors, when renting a holiday home.
- **Pack Essentials:** Be sure to include the necessities, like diapers, wipes, baby food, and any necessary prescriptions for your child. Overpacking on these requirements is frequently preferable.
- **Stroller and Baby Carrier:** Bring a stroller or baby carrier for convenient mobility, depending on your child's age. Consider using a baby carrier for older kids to explore places where a stroller might not be suitable.
- **Snacks and drink:** Keep youngsters nourished and hydrated by carrying a supply of snacks and drink, especially while going on trips.
- **First Aid:** Bring a first aid package that includes bandages, antiseptic wipes, and any special drugs your kid might need.

- **Plan Rest Break:** Children may require frequent breaks, particularly in the heat. To help them unwind, schedule rest stops in parks or tranquil locales.
- **Public Transportation:** Sydney's public transportation system is mainly kid-friendly. For simple transit on buses, trains, and ferries, think about getting an Opal card.
- **Look for child discounts:** Many attractions provide small children discounted or free entrance. For these reductions, check online or at the ticket counter.
- **Be adaptable:** Recognize that children have their own interests and speed. Keep an open mind while planning your day and provide time for unforeseen diversions or breaks.
- **Weather Preparedness:** Sydney's weather might change, so bring appropriate attire for the season. Sunscreen and hats are a must for sun protection.

- **Entertainment:** Bring leisure items like coloring books, crossword puzzles, or electronic gadgets with headphones for downtime.
- **Priority One:** Teach your children about street safety, including the need to look both ways. Moreover, have a strategy in case you become separated in busy areas.
- **Query Locals:** Never be afraid to seek advice or guidance from locals. They could be aware of less popular family-friendly locations.
- **Eat local food:** Introduce your kids to the cuisine of the area while still keeping some tried-and-true alternatives on hand for finicky eaters.

Keep in mind that traveling with children may be unpredictable, so keeping a good outlook and being adaptable are essential for a successful family trip to Sydney.

CHAPTER 10

Outdoor Adventure In Sydney

Beaches and Water Activities

Sydney is renowned for its stunning beaches and a variety of water sports. Here are a few well-liked choices:

Beaches

- **Bondi Beach**: Is well known for its fine sand and surfing scene. Swim, surf, or just lay down and soak up the sun.
- **Manly Beach:** Is another fantastic location for swimming, surfing, and seaside eating and is easily reachable by ferry.

- **Coogee Beach:** Families will love Coogee Beach, which has a beachfront promenade and ocean pools for secure swimming.
- **Bronte Beach:** Smaller and more sedate Bronte Beach has a natural ocean pool that's ideal for a tranquil swim.
- **Palm Beach:** A little farther north, Palm Beach is renowned for its unspoiled beauty and is ideal for picnics and swimming.

Activity in the Water

For surfers of all abilities, Sydney's beaches provide fantastic waves. Numerous surf schools provide training and equipment rentals.

- **Snorkeling and diving:** Visit locations like Shelly Beach, Clovelly, and Bare Island to explore the underwater world. You may join guided trips and hire equipment.

- **Kayaking:** For a different perspective of the city's shoreline, paddle around Sydney Harbor, Middle Harbor, or Pittwater.
- **Whale Watching**: From May to November, take a whale-watching excursion to witness humpback whales as they migrate.
- **Jet skiing and wakeboarding:** Several spots in Sydney provide jet ski rentals and wakeboarding opportunities.
- **Sailing:** To see the harbor's splendor from the water, join a sailing trip or hire a sailboat.
- **Fishing:** Sydney has excellent offshore and in the harbor fishing locations. You may throw your line from several wharves or sign up for a fishing trip.
- **Paddleboarding:** On calm bays and beaches around Sydney, try stand-up paddleboarding.
- **Swimming in Ocean Pools:** Take advantage of the special opportunity to swim in ocean pools like the Bondi Icebergs Pool and Bronte Baths.

Everyone can find something to enjoy on Sydney's beaches and in the sea, whether they're seeking adventure or leisures.

Hiking and Nature Reserves in Sydney

Sydney has numerous stunning hiking trails and natural areas. Here are a few well-liked choices:

- **National Park Royal:** It's the second-oldest national park in the world, and it's close to Sydney. There are several walking paths, such as the shore Track, which provides breathtaking views of the shore.
- **Blue Mountains National Park:** A little farther west lies the Blue Mountains National Park, which is renowned for its striking scenery and the Three Sisters rock formation. There are several paths and vantage points to discover.

- **Ku-ring-gai Chase National Park:** This park, which is in the north, offers both bushwalking opportunities and Aboriginal historical sites. Pittwater and the Pacific Ocean may be seen in amazing detail from the West Head overlook.

- **Garigal National Park:** Located to the north, it offers rich flora, including eucalypt trees and waterways, and is suitable for shorter excursions.
- **Botanic Gardens and Centennial:** Despite not being typical hiking destinations, Sydney's Botanic Gardens and Centennial Parklands provide tranquil strolls in the countryside.

- **Manly Scenic Walkway:** This coastal walk, which departs from Manly Wharf, provides beautiful views of Sydney Harbor, beaches, and lush greenery.

Before you travel, don't forget to verify the trail conditions, park policies, and any fire prohibitions as these might vary with the seasons. Enjoy Sydney's outdoor activities!

Affordable Activities and Eateries

Sydney might be costly, but there are still many inexpensive things to do and places to dine. Here are a few ideas:

Budget-friendly Activities
- **Beaches:** Bondi, Manly, and Coogee are just a few of Sydney's numerous, exquisitely maintained free beaches. Without paying any money, you may swim, sunbathe, or go on walks along the coast.

- **Botanic Gardens:** The Royal Botanic Garden in Sydney, which offers a tranquil haven in the middle of the city, is open to visitors without charge.

- **Markets:** For cheap shopping and street cuisine, check out the many markets including Paddy's Markets, Glebe Markets, or Bondi Markets.

- **Art Galleries:** The permanent collection is free to the general public at the Art Gallery of New South Wales.

- **Hiking: As** previously said, hiking in areas like Royal National Park or Ku-ring-gai Chase National Park is an inexpensive way to take in the natural surroundings.

Inexpensive Restaurants:

- **Food Courts:** For a variety of reasonably priced dining alternatives, head to the food courts in shopping centers like Westfield Sydney or World Square.

- **Chinatown:** Haymarket in Sydney is home to a large number of street food vendors and inexpensive eateries.

- **Local cafés:** Look around cheap local cafes that serve wonderful coffee and food in areas like Newtown or Surry Hills.

- **Food trucks:** Keep a look out for them, especially at well-known locales like Circular Quay and The Rocks. Pop-up markets are also a good idea.

- **BYO Restaurants:** To save money on drinks, look for eateries that let you bring your own wine (BYO).

- **Pub Food:** Many pubs serve hearty, reasonably priced pub food, such as traditional Australian fare like fish and chips and chicken schnitzel.

- **Student Discount:** Student discounts are available at a number of restaurants and attractions if you're a student.

Keep in mind that eating during lunch is frequently less expensive than doing so in the evening. You can find some hidden treasures that won't break the wallet by exploring your area and trying out various cuisines.

Free or Low-Cost Attractions

There are several free or inexpensive attractions in Sydney, Australia, that are geared toward a variety of interests. Here is a deeper look at some of the city's easiest-to-access and least-expensive activities:

- **Sydney Opera House:** While Sydney Opera House performance tickets might be rather expensive, you can still see this architectural marvel from the outside.

The Opera House is a must-see landmark due to its distinctive architecture and breathtaking waterfront setting.

- **Sydney Harbour Bridge:** Take in the breath-taking vistas of the city and the harbor by crossing the bridge on foot. It's a great way to take in the cityscape and take some priceless pictures.
- **Bondi to Coogee Coastal Walk:** The picturesque Bondi to Coogee Coastal Walk shows Sydney's unspoiled splendor and is totally free. Beautiful beaches, cliffs, and ocean pools can be seen throughout the route, which is ideal for a leisurely stroll or jog.
- **Royal Botanic Garden:** The Royal Botanic Garden is a tranquil retreat from the bustle of the city located right in the middle of it. It's free to stroll through the verdant landscape, look for local species, and take in the expansive views of the bay.

- **Art Gallery of New South Wales:** The world-renowned Art Gallery of New South Wales offers free pubic entry to its sizable collection of works by Australian and foreign artists that span decades.
- **Museum of Contemporary Art(MCA):** The Museum of Contemporary Art (MCA), another treasure of Sydney's art scene, grants free admission to all of its current shows. It's a fantastic location to discover contemporary innovation and art.
- **Sydney Beaches:** Enjoy the surf and sunshine at well-known beaches like Bondi, Manly, or Coogee in Sydney. Free activities include swimming and, if you have your own equipment, snorkeling.
- **Ferry Rides:** Although not completely free, catching a ferry is a cheap way to see Sydney Harbour. The Sydney Opera House, Harbour Bridge, and skyline vistas make the fare worthwhile.

- **The Rocks:** With its cobblestone walkways, artisan markets, and outdoor concerts,

this ancient district has a distinctive feel. On a self-guided walking tour, you may learn more about its history, or you can just enjoy the atmosphere.

- **Hyde Park:** Is a calm sanctuary in the middle of the city where you may unwind, enjoy a picnic, or wander among exquisitely planted gardens.

Sydney is now a budget-friendly vacation option because of these free or inexpensive attractions, which also provide a wide range of experiences that highlight the city's natural beauty, culture, and history.

CONCLUSION

Travelers are drawn to Sydney, Australia, by its unrivaled combination of scenic beauty, famous sites, and dynamic culture. The city continues to wow tourists with its world-famous beaches, including the vibrant coastlines of Bondi and the tranquil lengths of Manly, as we look ahead to the 2023–2024 tourism season. Water sports fans may enjoy a playground in Sydney's clear seas, from surfers riding the waves to snorkelers discovering vibrant underwater habitats.

Sydney offers a diverse range of activities in addition to its seaside attractiveness. While the Sydney Harbour Bridge enables you to stroll among expansive views, the Sydney Opera House stands as a tribute to architectural brilliance. Insights into the city's varied background may be found in its botanical gardens, art galleries, and historic areas like The Rocks.

Your traveling companion as you discover Sydney's mysteries is this travel guide. Sydney encourages you to explore its wonders in the forthcoming vacation season, whether you're drawn to exhilarating maritime excursions, cultural discoveries in its museums, or just lounging in the sun on golden beaches.

So be ready to make memories in Sydney, where every minute is an opportunity to immerse yourself in the beauty, culture, and adventure that this renowned Australian city has to offer in 2023–2024. Pack your luggage, make your schedule, and get ready to go. Travel safely!

SYDNEY:
1. BRIDGE CLIMB
2. OPERA HOUSE
3. DARLIN HARBOUR
4. ROCKS
5. LUNA PARK
6. ZOO - TORONGA
7. BONDI BEACH
8. BOTANIC GARDENS
9. HUNTER VALLEY WINE REGION

Printed in Great Britain
by Amazon